LORRIES

1890s TO 1970s

Nick Baldwin

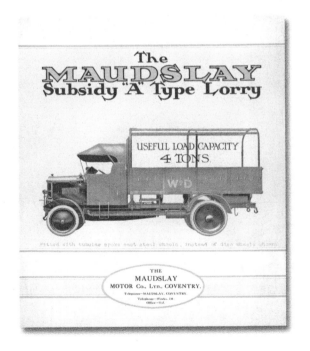

SHIRE PUBLICATIONS

Published by Shire Publications Ltd,
PO Box 883, Oxford, OX1 9PL, UK
PO Box 3985, New York, NY 10185-3985, USA
Email: shire@shirebooks.co.uk   www.shirebooks.co.uk

First published 2010.
Transferred to digital print on demand 2014.

Every attempt has been made by the Publishers to secure
the appropriate permissions for materials reproduced in
this book. If there has been any oversight we will be happy
to rectify the situation and a written submission should be
made to the Publishers.

A CIP catalogue record for this book is available from the
British Library.

Shire Library no. 578   •   ISBN-13: 978 0 74780 755 1

Nick Baldwin has asserted his right under the Copyright,
Designs and Patents Act, 1988, to be identified as the
author of this book.

Designed by Tony Truscott Designs, Sussex, UK
Typeset in Perpetua and Gill Sans.
Printed and bound in Great Britain.

COVER IMAGE
Cover design by Peter Ashley. Front cover: 1951 AEC
Mammoth Major Mk. III, photograph by Nick Wright.
Back cover: Bedford TK badge, photograph by
Nick Wright.

TITLE PAGE IMAGE
Maudslay, with help from their Coventry neighbours
Rover, made some two thousand subsidy lorries. They
were unusual in featuring overhead camshaft motors.

CONTENTS PAGE IMAGE
As well as selling fruit, Hickman's J-type Thornycroft
could transport furniture 100 miles per day – showing the
very limited range on solid tyres at the 12-mph legal speed
of the day.

Shire Publications is supporting the Woodland Trust, the UK's leading woodland conservation charity, by funding the dedication of trees.

CONTENTS

STEAM, ELECTRICITY OR PETROL?   4

GROWTH, CONSOLIDATION AND NEW IDEAS   10

THE SPREAD OF DIESEL   20

HIGHS AND LOWS: 1940–69   30

LOADS OF POWER IN EUROPE   42

INDEX   56

STEAM, ELECTRICITY OR PETROL?

UNTIL 1896 the horse remained unchallenged for all Britain's road transport needs. Steam railways handled the long-distance transport of goods, but steam had made few inroads on the highway. Traction engines and trailers had been used for the big castings and fabrications of Victorian industry but from 1865 they had been severely restricted – for example, they were permitted to travel at only 4 mph, or half that in built-up areas.

In 1896 the rules were relaxed, providing that unladen weight was less than 3 tons, or 4 tons with trailer. Then 14 mph was permissible, though the law instructed that vehicles 'should be so constructed that no smoke or visible vapour be emitted except from any temporary or accidental cause'.

By then marine engineers Thornycroft had built steam 'lurries' (as early lorries were called) to carry rather than pull loads, but weight and vapour were problematical. In 1898, some twenty years before the use of semi-trailers became widespread, they built an articulated steam lorry.

Meanwhile the recently invented internal combustion engine had been applied to automobiles on the Continent, and in 1893 to the first load-carrier, a waggonette from Panhard & Levassor. This was followed by a van from Benz in 1894, and heavier lorries from Daimler two years later. From 1897 the Daimler licensee in Coventry built its own commercial vehicles and other British pioneers soon joined them.

For local deliveries, battery-electric vehicles proved to be the simplest to operate and the easiest on which to train drivers, and ways began to be found to expand the range by creating hybrids. These had internal combustion engines powering dynamos feeding traction motors. Several firms tried these ideas but the only notable commercial success was enjoyed by W. A. Stevens from 1908, initially based on Hallford lorries. Hallford petrol-driven lorries were new in 1907 from an old-established engineering firm and were based on Swiss Saurer designs. Production lasted to 1925 but from 1911 Stevens built his own vehicles and gained backing from transport operator Thomas Tilling – hence the name Tilling-Stevens for the vehicles.

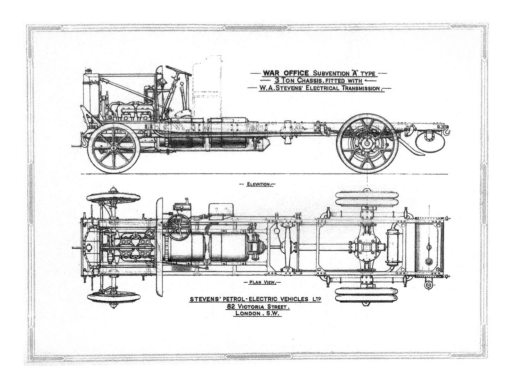

Trials took place to explore the relative merits of particular types and makes of vehicle, the most important early example being the Lancashire Heavy Motor Vehicle Trials organised by the Liverpool Self-Propelled Traffic Association in 1898, 1899 and 1901. They were dominated by steam and were followed in 1901 by War Office trials at Aldershot, where steam won the three premier awards. Numerous other events followed, culminating in the 1907 RAC trials, where steam was found to be the best for loads of over 3 tons, and petrol internal combustion for lower weights. The heavy vehicles were limited to 5 mph on steel tyres and 8 mph on solid rubber, but vehicles under 3 tons unladen on rubber tyres could travel at 12 mph, which gave some incentive for operators to buy these more efficient and less road-damaging vehicles.

Although internal combustion vehicles are loosely referred to as 'petrol-driven', many of them could be switched to run on the cheaper paraffin once warm. Likewise, while most steam vehicles ran on coal or coke, some like the Lifu at the Lancashire Trials relied on liquid fuel (hence the name).

All types of vehicle tended to have final drive by chains, though exceptions included the German Daimler, sold in Britain by tramcar maker

W.A. Stevens was involved with petrol-electric vehicles at Hallford from 1908, and later at Tilling-Stevens and Dennis. Tilling-Stevens also made battery-electrics sporadically between 1914 and 1950. This 1910s Dennis has the generator ahead of the traction motor.

A Leyland laden with bags of wool stands outside Fox Bros cloth mill, much of which still stands, in Wellington, Somerset, in the late 1890s.

Heavy vehicle trials, such as these in France in 1906, created enormous interest and favourable publicity for the new lorries.

G. F. Milnes under the name Milnes-Daimler, which had shaft drive with internal ring gearing in the wheels. Shaft and worm drive proved to be a mechanically efficient and quiet way to transmit power and was adopted gradually by much of the industry following the lead of Dennis in 1904. Internal combustion engines had two or four cylinders cast individually or in pairs, and the three or four gears had difficult-to-engage sliding mesh, though

a few, such as Commer Cars, had constant mesh with dog-clutch engagement. By then Thornycroft had all but abandoned steam, and Leyland (which began as the Lancashire Steam Motor Company) put most emphasis on internal combustion while keeping a steam department operating on a small scale into the 1920s.

Foden's steam dominance was challenged by newcomer Sentinel in 1906 and there were numerous other steam-vehicle makers, often originating from Victorian agricultural engineers such as Burrell, Fowler, Clayton & Shuttleworth, Garrett and Robey.

A railway container carried by a Thornycroft steam wagon, with minimal protection for the driver.

New requirements for registration and licensing, which introduced number plates, showed that there were four thousand goods vehicles in use in Britain in 1904 and this figure had reached forty thousand in 1911, of which perhaps a quarter were steam-powered.

The earlier military trials had helped the War Office arrive at a specification for a petrol-engined 3-tonner ideal for its requirements. It offered a subsidy to civilian operators to buy vehicles that in the event of call-up would be bought at an agreed price. Only about a hundred vehicles were registered under this scheme in 1911 but, as more were added, it at least increased the availability of well-designed vehicles with standardised layout of driving controls.

A steel-tyred Milnes-Daimler, with ring gear drive to the rear wheels, working for a brewer in 1903.

In general, the only firms able to afford the pre-war vehicles had been wealthy brewers, colliers, laundries, weavers and spinners, engineers and manufacturers, while the traditional cartage contractors (with the notable exception of Pickfords) continued to make do with horses or traction engines.

Brewers helped to account for the success of Dennis in Guildford, Commer in Luton and Thornycroft in Basingstoke, all areas that were outside the traditional North of England heavy-manufacturing centres.

7

Petrol lorries tended to have bonnets but Karrier and a few others increased load space by placing the driver over the engine, as on this Scottish-built 1907 Argyll 2-tonner.

Napier, a London precision engineering firm that had made banknote machinery, became a maker of cars, and then of commercial vehicles. This oil-lit one-tonner dates from about 1908.

The Ryknield lorry from Burton-upon-Trent was sponsored by members of the Bass brewing family.

While the new motor industry that grew from bicycle manufacture in Coventry and Birmingham spawned numerous motorcycle and car firms, it produced few heavy-vehicle makers of note, apart from Austin, Maudslay and, briefly, Wolseley. A significant newcomer in 1914 at Wolverhampton was Guy, founded by Sunbeam's former works manager Sidney Guy.

This 1912 Commer (the 'Cars' part of the name soon disappeared from the radiator script) averaged 14.7 miles per gallon when delivering whisky. The rear chain cases were oil-filled and the gearbox was an easy-change Linley preselector.

Commer Cars made by the Commercial Car Company of Luton for work in foreign lands.

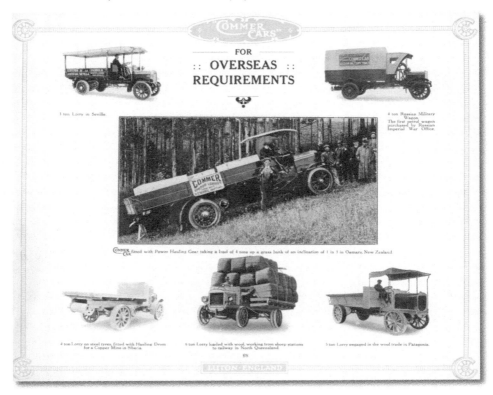

9

GROWTH, CONSOLIDATION AND NEW IDEAS

B ETWEEN the outbreak of war in 1914 and its end in 1918 some 37,000 lorries were built in Britain for the military authorities. Tens of thousands more were purchased from the United States, including many with four-wheel drive made by Nash, Jeffery and FWD. In 1918 Nash built 11,490 of its Quads, a world record at the time.

The most prolific British producer of lorries proved to be AEC, the builder of London's buses. Its moving-track assembly lines conceived on American principles turned out over ten thousand Y-type 3-tonners, some of which were supplied as Daimlers with that Coventry firm's engines. Thornycroft, Dennis, Albion, Commer and Leyland each produced several thousand vehicles, and smaller numbers came from Maudslay, Karrier, Hallford and others. By and large they performed admirably in appalling conditions, and their survivors went on to be the backbone of the civilian transport companies that were set up after the war by hundreds of military-trained drivers.

Leyland was worried that these war-surplus vehicles would damage its new-vehicle sales, and it set about buying back so-called RAF-type Leylands and reconditioning some three thousand of them (about half the total built), so that they would not harm an already enviable reputation and become too cheap. After a brief flurry of new vehicle orders, the war-surplus vehicles weakened all their makers for several years but at least they enabled new haulage firms to enter the business at modest cost.

In 1919 the Ministry of Transport was established and the following year it classified roads as A or B grade and introduced the Road Fund Licence, which began to tax goods vehicles more heavily and discriminate gradually against those that were claimed to do most damage to roads.

The 62,000 registered heavy vehicles on British roads in 1919 had grown to 236,000 in 1925 (many of them American ex-War Department types) and 355,000 in 1930, by which time most of the war-surplus types had expired. Apart from the Leylands, these old lorries had come in for extensive rebuilding and, like new vehicles, they had begun to be fitted with pneumatic

Opposite:
The first J-type Thornycroft joined the Pickfords fleet in 1913, and five thousand were supplied for the war effort. The model continued in production at Basingstoke until 1927. This is a 1922 sales brochure cover.

Albions coping
with familiar
gradients, but here
in the Khyber Pass,
rather than their
native Scotland.

tyres in the middle of the decade, along with weatherproof cabs. The
reconditioning of three of the American makes created new British firms
around London, the British FWD and Peerless, and the Gilford from a
former Garford specialist. As surplus American parts and engines ran out,
they were fitted with locally sourced components. FWD became AEC's
specialist off-road vehicles division in 1929 and within ten years had created
the renowned Matador military 4x4 of the Second World War.

Large numbers of vehicles were imported from the United States and
Europe in the 1920s. These were particularly damaging to the British car and
van industry but included a significant number of lorries. Having
experimented with various levels of import duty, the government eventually
imposed a surcharge of a third of the value of imported vehicles in May 1926;
this encouraged Dodge and General Motors to establish factories in Britain,
alongside Ford, which had been assembling cars and light commercials at
Trafford Park, Manchester, since 1911. Several firms converted these Model
Ts by fitting heavier frames, additional gearboxes and heavy-duty rear axles
and wheels, or by adding semi-trailers to enable them to carry 1–3 tons.

Articulated vehicles had been understood since Victorian times but did
not achieve sales success until Carrimore and Scammell began to make
matched artics at the end of the First World War. Carrimore favoured
Leyland tractive units, while Scammell, with
London coachbuilding origins, introduced
a complete 8- to 15-

A First World War
military line-up
with Scottish
Halleys flanking an
American Bulldog
Mack and a Ford
Model T to the
right.

FWDs came in for numerous conversions over the years. Here a 4x4 is shown fitted with Roadless half-tracks, an idea first tried by the Royal National Lifeboat Institution in 1929.

tonner from a new factory at Watford. Beardmore made a cross between a road tractor hauling a drawbar trailer and an artic by incorporating an attachment point that could be raised to lift the front trailer wheels for unladen running. This idea came from Chenard-Walcker in France and allowed the unballasted tractor to be taxed more cheaply than a heavy artic. Another idea from France was the front-wheel-drive Latil, allowing very low body height at the rear. Latil had pioneered front-wheel drive in 1898 but became best-known in Britain in the 1930s with 4x4 and four-wheel-steered

An unusual mid-1920s use for a pair of American Liberty lorries. They are hauling a 20-ton boiler, with one travelling backwards.

An advertising card for the 1926 Karrier CY6 2½-ton-capacity six-wheeler with double-drive tandem and 25-hp four-cylinder petrol engine. Primarily a military vehicle, it was also sold to civil engineers and for colonial on/off-road duties.

tractors licence-built by low-loader specialists Shelvoke & Drewry (S&D). Small-wheeled low-loaders with rear-wheel drive were in vogue at the time with such firms as S&D, Easyloader and Vulcan.

In the world of competitively priced cars, Morris had become the largest British producer in the early 1920s. Morris introduced its 1-tonner in 1924, soon after its severely weakened rival Austin bowed out of the lorry market to concentrate on the small cars that would revive it.

Coachbuilder's plate showing the layout of a hand-operated screw tipper on a 1926 chassis loosely based on the new Morris-Commercial.

The Morris 1-tonner soon outsold all other light lorries, with over 25,000 produced to the end of 1930, and was joined by larger models, including rigid six-wheelers, an idea pioneered in the United States in the early 1920s. By 1924 the Californian Moreland six-wheeler achieved a notable first: Lockheed hydraulic brakes with Westinghouse air assistance. Adding a third axle under the load space became a popular way of increasing payload on many makes of vehicle from the mid-1920s and, while it induced tyre scrub when cornering on solid-tyred lorries, the more flexible pneumatics were less susceptible. The simplest six-wheelers had trailing axles, but double-drive tandems came to be fitted to military types and had spread to regular road haulage by 1930.

While Morris-Commercial was

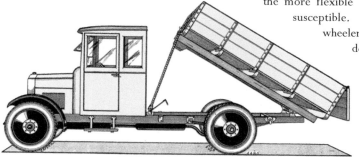

mass-producing small commercials (a route adopted less successfully by other car rivals such as Singer and Bean), larger types were hand-built in small batches by several dozen specialist manufacturers. AEC was concentrating primarily on its buses and, like Leyland, would not come up with a complete range of lorries incorporating all the latest ideas until 1929.

Specifications evolved during the 1920s to include monobloc engines mounted in unit with the previously separate gearboxes. They mostly gained overhead valves, and their cone clutches gave way to plate types. Six-cylinder engines, as introduced by Halley in 1920, were viewed with suspicion by operators as they had previously been the preserve of fire appliances and export specials and, to begin with, were perceived to be complex, thirsty and too refined for hard work. However, by the late 1920s many commercials had six cylinders and they also featured braked front axles in addition to the transmission and rear-wheel brakes of their forebears. Four-speed gearboxes were beginning to have dual-ratio transfer boxes to multiply ratios, and cabs now featured safety glass all round. Chain drive had been finally ousted on all but the heaviest Scammells and their like.

Bonneted layouts were gradually replaced by forward control but this led to engine-access difficulties, which AEC endeavoured to address with a

The semi-trailer was initially permanently attached to the tractor in the chain-driven Scammell artic. The 1928 Southern Roadways example in the foreground had the operator's name picked out in reflective glass studs.

hinged-back upper cab in 1929. True tilt cabs had been invented by Lauth-Juergens in the United States in 1911 but did not arrive in Britain until after the Second World War.

After the post-war doldrums, commercial vehicle production (including buses and coaches) reached 23,604 in 1923, 35,000 in 1925, 47,227 in 1927 and 66,859 in 1930, with some 10 per cent of the last figure going for export.

The industry was evolving, with a number of the early leaders succumbing to progress and others being drawn into new groupings. Commer had struggled to adapt to post-war conditions and in 1925 was bought by Humber, which in turn became a cornerstone of the Rootes Group, along with Hillman. Guy acquired its near neighbour Star for expansion. AEC, with its ties to the London bus monopoly, tried to increase its sales to outside operators by closer links with Daimler. The Associated Daimler Company (ADC) existed from 1926 to 1928, and during this period AEC moved its production facilities from Walthamstow to well-equipped new premises at Southall. After Daimler and AEC went their separate ways, AEC became independent of the London Underground and bus operation in 1933, though it retained a ten-year contract to build 90 per cent of London's

Horses still played their part in station deliveries when this forward-control Karrier and normal-control AEC Y type worked for the London Midland & Scottish Railway.

bus requirements. Both Leyland and Ford had declined to purchase the AEC business at the time.

The once-important Scottish commercial-vehicle industry dwindled to just Albion and Halley, the latter's factory being acquired by Albion in 1935. Caledon, which had been started by the Scottish Commer distributor during the war, flourished briefly but ended up as an offshoot of Suffolk steam engineers Garrett in the mid-1920s.

Beardmore moved its vehicle production to London, while Sentinel, originally from Glasgow, had built its steam vehicles in Shrewsbury since 1917 to be nearer its principal English market. Most of the other steam-lorry manufacturers fell by the wayside following declining sales. Garrett and Ransomes both tried to compensate by offering electric vehicles, but sales were small in the 1920s and 1930s. The Ransomes electrics were known as 'Orwell', a reference to the local river rather than to the author of *1984*.

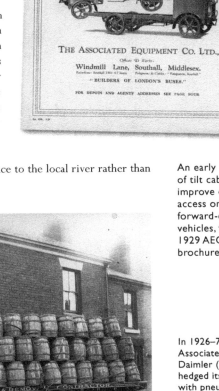

An early example of tilt cab to improve engine access on forward-control vehicles, from a 1929 AEC brochure cover.

In 1926–7 Associated Daimler (ADC) hedged its bets, with pneumatic tyres on the steered wheels and solid tyres at the heavy end – a common layout at the time because of worries about punctures.

Above: Petrol and steam road tractors were popular. This Foden carries a 1928 Manchester registration plate and has a horizontal boiler, unlike the vertical Sentinel layout.

Below: A Sentinel steam waggon (only Sentinel used this spelling) has come to grief, much to the amusement of the onlookers.

Operated in the livery of Tanqueray Gordon, this 1927 Leyland actually belonged to haulage contractors Chas A. Wells, which became part of British Road Services in the 1940s.

Although they were ideal for local deliveries, by 1930 it was rare to find battery-electric vehicles as large as this Birmingham-built GV. Battery-electrics by then tended to be milk floats, though Garrett and Ransomes also made larger types. Thirsty petrol-electrics had all but died out.

THE NEW
Leyland
'OCTOPUS'
EIGHT
WHEELER

A popular model for trunk-road service—an oil-engine long-wheelbase Octopus, with trailing-axle bogie.

Leyland Motors Ltd

THE SPREAD OF DIESEL

THE 1930s were an era of government intervention into the free-for-all of road transport, and there were dramatic changes to vehicles and the way in which they operated.

The 1930–4 Road Traffic Acts brought in driving-hours restrictions and third-party insurance, construction laws covering dimensions and weights (12 tons gross on two axles, 13 if steam powered; 19 tons on three axles and 22 tons on more than three axles or with a trailer), turning circle, brakes, tyres (solids only on heavy road transport locomotives and tractors), safety glass, speed (20 mph for heavy motor cars and 30 mph for others including in built-up areas), lighting, marking with the operator's address and, from 1933, the need for special operators' licences. These were 'A' licences for carriers of other people's freight, cheaper 'B' licences for hauliers carrying a proportion of their own goods, and 'C' licences for manufacturers and producers delivering their own goods. The *News Chronicle*'s guide booklet comprised 112 tightly packed pages, confirming that this was complex and draconian legislation. It was based on a report to Parliament by the railway-biased Salter Committee and was plainly intended to protect the railway companies from unregulated road haulage. Not that the railway companies had been slow to enter the market: they had four thousand lorries in use by 1929, in contrast to almost twenty thousand horses and more than 32,000 trailers. Ten years later the figures were 10,728, 12,106 and 24,615 respectively.

Drivers were limited to five-and-a-half-hour spells at the wheel before enforced rest, and transport cafés sprang up beside trunk routes to cater for them. 'Spy in the cab' tachographs to monitor hours appeared in Germany around 1930 but did not become compulsory in Britain until 1982.

Fuel duty was levied on petrol, and the extra costs incurred by the reduction in hours and the A licence, to say nothing of numerous other restrictions, made road haulage in the recession of that time an extremely parlous business.

Opposite:
A 1935 sales brochure cover for the 22-ton gross Octopus with six-cylinder petrol or oil engines, four-speed gearbox and servo brakes on all but the second set of steered wheels.

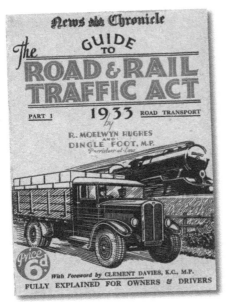

The *News Chronicle* issued this 112-page booklet in an attempt to explain the intricacies of the 1933 Road and Rail Traffic Act, which had been influenced by railway company interests.

However, there was an important saviour on the horizon, and that was the diesel engine. Diesels were named after their German inventor, Dr Rudolf Diesel, but were often known in Britain as 'heavy oil engines', as an Englishman, Herbert Ackroyd Stuart, held Victorian patents, so the German name seemed inappropriate to many.

Early diesels were heavy in relation to power output and were primarily for marine and industrial applications. However, in the early 1920s a flurry of activity took place in France, Switzerland and Germany to produce diesel vehicles. By the late 1920s they were available in several German chassis and in Swiss Saurers. A Mercedes-Benz chassis was exhibited at the 1927 London Commercial Motor Show and a few orders were taken, the pound-to-deutschmark currency ratio being advantageous to the British at the time.

Saurer's very well-engineered petrol-engined chassis were well known in Britain following their early adoption by Hallford, and, with the success of Saurer's 1928 diesels, Sir W. G. Armstrong-Whitworth & Company, a respected Tyneside shipbuilder and engineer, acquired a licence and offered Armstrong-Saurers from 1931.

AEC had its own diesel on trial in the late 1920s, but most interest was taken in the Gardner marine engine, which was tried in a few conversions of previously petrol chassis. Finally Walker Brothers of Wigan took the plunge and in 1930 offered the Gardner as standard in one of their little-known Pagefield chassis. The extreme economy of this engine encouraged Foden to adopt the same type of engine in 1931, though it was reluctant to withdraw from steam and came up with increasingly complex and costly designs into

Mercedes-Benz sales were helped in Britain by the weak deutschmark and the availability of diesels. This is a 1932 6/7-tonner with 85-bhp six-cylinder 8½-litre motor.

The Samson 15-ton rigid eight was new from Armstrong-Saurer in 1934, the same year in which AEC's better-known Mammoth Major 8 took to the road.

1932. Soon Gardners were available in several makes of chassis, particularly when the LW (lightweight) automotive, as opposed to marine, type became available in August 1931. The original L had been available in one- to six-cylinder forms and it was found with the longer LW that a three-cylinder 3LW unit was usually all that could fit in a bay designed for a four-cylinder petrol engine, and likewise a 5LW in place of a six.

Other steam-vehicle makers fared less well than Foden, despite Garrett having been a diesel pioneer in 1928 using McLaren-Benz engines. It also supplied a Caledon chassis to Aveling & Porter to receive one of its Invicta oil engines. However, both firms were in a parlous state and few orders were taken.

Railway engineers Kerr Stuart tried a Helios engine and then specified McLaren-Benz in 1929, before collapsing a year later, having built only five lorries. One of the most famed of all the steam-based enterprises was Fowler of Leeds, which offered heavy oil lorries from 1931 with its own engines, but had been forced to adopt Gardners by the time it bowed out in 1935. By then its neighbour at Hunslet, the Yorkshire Patent Steam Wagon Company, was also making Dorman-Ricardo oil-engined lorries, but even the adoption of Gardners did not make its assembled vehicles competitive on price, and the firm concentrated on specialist tankers and municipal bodywork after 1938.

Atkinson was another North of England steam-lorry maker to have hit hard times. It had acquired Leyland's steam spares in 1926 and the defunct Mann Steam Wagon & Cart Company in 1929 but was little more than a garage by 1931, eking out an existence by adding axles or pneumatic tyres to old vehicles. The fitting of diesel engines became an important sideline and soon it was assembling new diesel lorries employing Blackstone, Tangye, Dorman and other engines. Two London businessmen saw the potential and acquired the business, coming up with the ideal specification for an assembled lorry of Gardner diesel, David Brown gearbox and Kirkstall axles – all components made in the North of England.

A similar formula was adopted by E. R. Foden, who had retired from the Foden family firm because of its reluctance to put all its resources behind its 1931 diesel lorry. He came out of retirement at the age of sixty-one and in 1933 came up with the first diesel lorry that could carry 7½ tons yet weigh under 4 tons unladen.It bore his ERF initials after a brief period as E. R. Foden.

Meanwhile Sentinel alone remained true to steam, producing some highly sophisticated designs, but was rewarded with registrations of only 168 vehicles in 1934 and thirty in 1935. It pioneered rigid eight-wheelers in 1929, an idea adopted by AEC in diesel form for its Mammoth Major of 1934. In a desperate attempt to remain in business, Sentinel acquired Garner in 1934 and offered its petrol- and diesel-engined vehicles as Sentinel-Garners. However, they did not make happy bedfellows and some former Chrysler-Dodge employees took Garner to a new independent existence in north London in 1936. Sentinel made a few steam vehicles right through to the early 1950s, while diversifying into other fields. In 1938 Sentinel built some prototype vehicles running on producer gas, to the design of HSG, but, though the idea of making gas from wood or fossil fuels became viable in the liquid-fuel shortages of the Second World War, it did not benefit Sentinel. This was particularly poignant in view of the firm's claim in 1933 that each of its vehicles would keep two British miners in work.

HSG was successor to Gilford, which had been making American-powered and inspired fast and competitively priced commercial chassis

Launched in 1933, the S-model shaft-driven steam Sentinel was competitive with the new petrol and diesel Leylands, like the Beaver on the left. Behind is a Shelvoke & Drewry low-loader.

(mostly for passengers) since the mid-1920s but had succumbed when its rivals caught up with its specifications in the 1930s.

The far higher compression ratios of diesels compared with petrol units helped to give them higher thermal efficiency and frugal fuel consumption, and diesel fuel was cheaper than petrol, even when taxed.

One of the most significant developments was the arrival of Frank Perkins's diesels in 1932. He had been works director at road-roller maker Barford & Perkins and, working with Charles Chapman, formerly of Beardmore and Petter engines, he reasoned that lighter diesels, able to exceed the narrow rev band of traditional diesels, would be more compatible with petrol-engined vehicles. One of the few lorries to use the Petter two-stroke diesels was the Shefflex, whose origins went back to luxury cars and making copies of 2-ton Commers in the First World War. As it was, only the maximum-weight lorries benefited from the big diesels, and smaller ones powered by two- or three-cylinder Gardners (or, indeed, Petters) were rough and difficult to drive. When they were installed in chassis designed for petrol engines, the top speed could be cut in half because of lower engine revs, so transmission ratios had to be changed.

Perkins put an end to all that with four-cylinder diesels compatible with petrol units. It then, in 1937, introduced its more powerful six-cylinder P6, which became the backbone of many transport fleets up to the 1960s. As volumes increased, prices fell, and even the newly developed medium-weight

Gilford lorries tended to use six-cylinder American engines (some copied by Coventry Climax, though Gilford also favoured Meadows petrol units when this tanker was sold in 1931).

An early Bedford with trailing axle conversion and Eagle water-spraying equipment for an export customer.

Commer lorries of the Rootes Group, conceived for mass production, could be supplied in Perkins diesel form from 1933 at competitive prices.

Commer had become a mainstream manufacturer like Morris-Commercial and both had the new American-transplant Dodges and Chevrolets to contend with. The latter were rebranded 'Bedford' in 1931 and were built by General Motors' Vauxhall subsidiary. Although initially catering only for the lighter end of the market, Bedford had captured a quarter of all British commercial-vehicle sales within six years, and up to half of exports. It was slow to move into the medium and heavyweight range and survived without a 1930s diesel option.

Dodge, or Kew Dodge as the British models were known after their area of manufacture, never enjoyed the success of Bedford but moved into heavier vehicles sooner and offered the P6 from 1938.

In the face of all this competition, Morris-Commercial redesigned its vehicles in line with the latest American ideas and introduced the four- and six-cylinder C types in 1933, followed by the CV of 1937. The last could in theory have become Saurer-powered, as Morris acquired a licence from the Swiss firm, but it had to put the project on hold until the end of the Second World War.

Morris-Commercial had tried a brave foray into the heavy-vehicle market in 1930 under new ex-AEC chief engineer C. K. Edwards. It offered two-axle buses and lorries up to 8 tons plus a 4/5 ton Courier and smaller Leaders. It was suggested that William Morris sanctioned this diversification to keep his skilled engineers at his recently acquired Wolseley factory occupied after the collapse of trade caused by the Wall Street Crash. Whatever his intentions, sales were disappointing and it took the C types to lift overall sales back to ten thousand per year after seven thousand in 1932, or around half that of the new Bedford.

A Commer Superpoise 3-tonner of 1939, the name denoting a wide axle spread to give correct weight distribution. Morris-Commercial's equivalent was called the Equiload.

The 2-ton Cub took Leyland into the mass market in 1931. It was said to have been unofficially based on Chrysler-Dodge designs.

Import duty, reduced demand and local manufacture had all contributed to falling imports (down from 16,250 in 1929 to 1,600 in 1934) and these were mostly cheap vans or popular American (or cheaper duty Canadian) 'speed trucks' like the Reo, or General Motors' cheap Opels. In the same period exports were eight thousand and almost fourteen thousand respectively and reached seventeen thousand in 1936. Britain was by then third only to the United States and the Soviet Union in terms of commercial

Albion had its own diesel available in 1933 but also used Gardners, as in this RL59 12-tonner weighing almost 7 tons unladen.

The cover of AEC's house magazine in 1931, showing one of the new range designed by John Rackham, who had previously worked on Leyland's competing vehicles.

VOL. VI. No. 7.
AUGUST. 1931.

AEC

Gazette

THE ASSOCIATED EQUIPMENT CO., LTD., SOUTHALL, MIDDX.

vehicles produced, the 112,769 of 1937 being almost double that of fourth-placed Germany and way ahead of France in fifth with 25,000.

AEC, Leyland, Thornycroft, Dennis, Albion and Guy were amongst the larger firms offering broad ranges of vehicles, but there were dozens of others specialising in particular niches. With its acquisition of Karrier in 1934, Rootes had an extensive range alongside its Commers, including the new Cob mechanical horses and an extensive assortment of municipal vehicles.

Scammell, too, had gone both up and down the weight ranges. It had taken over Napier's ideas for a three-wheel Mechanical Horse in 1932 and went on to sell some fourteen thousand of them by the outbreak of war, with around twice as many quickly detachable semi-trailers. They outnumbered other Scammells of the time by five to one, though most public interest was directed towards a massive 100-ton-capacity low-loader built in 1929 for carrying export locomotives to the docks. It relied on Scammell's 80-hp four-cylinder petrol engine and had high and low ranges for its four-speed gearbox. Its fuel consumption of 2 miles per gallon (mpg) was transformed to 4 mpg in 1932 by the fitment of a Gardner 6LW diesel. A second machine was built for hauling a stone crusher and it, too, was converted before passing

Scammell made its famous normal-control artics (centre), off-road and heavy haulage types, and the Mechanical Horses and rubber-suspended rigid eights illustrated.

ERF's first articulated vehicle of 1935, with Gardner 5LW. Foden had stopped ERF from spelling out 'E. R. Foden' in full on the radiator by this stage.

to Pickfords in 1934. Although the tractors appeared to have two conventional solid-tyred axles, the rear one actually consisted of two in line, each shod with twin double-tyred wheels, and each axle oscillating at its middle from the chassis and receiving separate drive by chain.

Relative newcomer ERF had entered the rigid-eight market in 1935 and also introduced a 5LW-powered articulated machine. It also used Gardner's new mid-weight lorry engine, the 4LK, in place of the 3LW, in its smallest 4-tonner. In 1937 ERF came up with the first twin-steer six-wheeler, a 9-tonner with 5LW diesel. Popularly known as 'Chinese six', this layout reduced tyre costs and became quite popular, being adopted by Leyland for its appropriately named Steer, a new member for its 'zoo' (and 'aquarium') of animal names, which also included the Octopus rigid eight.

Towards the end of the 1930s, firms such as Guy and Crossley switched to military production, and there were two important newcomers taking advantage of legislation that allowed lorries weighing less than 2½ tons to travel at 30 mph instead of 20 mph. Jensen made some massive vehicles for carrying Reynolds Tubes which just complied, owing to their unitary construction in aluminium alloy. After the war, the 6-ton JNSN, as it was badged, enjoyed considerable, albeit brief, success in general haulage.

The other newcomer was Seddon, which had roots in transport, lorry reconditioning and an agency for Reo trucks. It introduced a 6-tonner weighing under 2½ tons in 1938, incorporating the Perkins P6 diesel, and was soon making seven to eight per week.

In 1939 a familiar name returned to the scene. This was Austin, which had continued with car-derived vans but now decided to enter the mid-weight mass-produced field with its K series, closely based on contemporary Bedfords and widely, though unofficially, referred to as 'Birmingham Bedfords'.

HIGHS AND LOWS: 1940-69

A T THE outbreak of war in 1939, all motor factories switched to building military vehicles, aero engines, aircraft and parts, munitions, tracked machines and dozens of other projects for the war effort. What they achieved was celebrated in such post-war books as *Vital to the Life of the Nation* and *Drive for Freedom*. These told of AEC's production of over nine thousand 4x4 Matadors, plus many more types, as well as engines for Atkinson, Maudslay and others. Albion made a thousand tank transporters and there were two thousand Scammell Pioneer six-wheelers. Thornycroft added over five thousand 4x4 Nubians, plus sixteen other types of vehicle, including two thousand crane carriers; Guy, Daimler and the Rootes Group made thousands of armoured cars, while the Nuffield Organisation (owning Wolseley and Morris) made tanks and tens of thousands of other military vehicles. Indeed, there was not a lorry maker that did not make a major contribution, with Austin and Bedford leading in terms of numbers. Austin made 115,000 assorted military vehicles, and Bedford almost double that figure. Ironically, as part of General Motors, Bedford found its vehicles fighting similar ones made in Germany by Opel, though the balance was more than redressed by Chevrolet and GMC, the latter alone supplying some 560,000 of their famous 6x6 2½-tonner to the Allied war effort.

All this military might is outside the scope of this survey but had important repercussions in that the production capacity of the motor industry had been massively enlarged when it returned to peace. It also ensured that there was an enormous pool of ex-military lorries, just as there had been after the First World War. Again, these came in for all manner of conversion and modernisation in the later 1940s and into the 1950s.

During the conflict, the Ministry of War permitted production of lorries for essential civilian duties such as food and fuel transport, milk collection and delivery of raw materials to the factories. Notable in this field was Ford, whose lorries had been labelled 'Thames' since 1939. Many of these were V8 petrol-powered, as they had been since the mid-1930s, and, as well as lorries, Ford's Dagenham factory made 262,000 V8 engines for a variety of uses such

Opposite:
A 1960 Gardner advertisement showing examples of its beautifully engineered diesels (that had changed little in outward appearance in twenty-five years), and outlining their data, including their low governed revs, low power output but massive torque.

Since 1935 Ford had used V8 petrol engines in some models and since 1939 had called them 'Thames'. This is a 1942 7V tipper with blackout masks and visibility stripes.

A British Road Services Bedford with wartime austerity bonnet style in the late 1940s, on the type of work normally confined to local operators.

as Bren-gun carriers. Ford's factories were also massive wartime suppliers of vehicles and equipment.

The period from 1946 was one of enormous challenges for the lorry-manufacturing industry and for road haulage in general. The country was desperate for foreign exchange currency, having borrowed beyond its means during the war years. As a result the motor industry was exhorted to 'export or die'. Unfortunately, the German, Japanese and American industries had similar ideas, and what had been traditional British export markets began to disappear. To combat the scale of American industry, the British Government and some industry leaders wanted fewer and larger units. The process began in 1948 with the creation of Associated Commercial Vehicles (ACV), consisting primarily of AEC with the addition of Maudslay, Crossley, and bodywork and cab specialist Park Royal Vehicles. Crossley had built vehicles for the RAF but was mainly involved with buses, while Maudslay, following new ownership immediately before the war, had enjoyed a remarkable revival that saw its production increase to around one thousand per year from a wartime shadow factory established at Alcester in Warwickshire.

A 'Chinese six' Maudslay from a firm that had enjoyed a dramatic revival since 1938 and had joined AEC in 1948, when this tipper was built.

The next major development occurred when Leyland bought Albion in 1951, and then came the far-reaching amalgamation of Austin and Morris and all their associates into the British Motor Corporation (BMC) in 1952–3. In 1955 Leyland added Scammell to its portfolio. AEC countered by buying Thornycroft's vehicle business in 1961 and then merging with Leyland in the following year.

The creation of BMC opened up an era of 'badge-engineered' Austin and Morris vehicles of identical specification, many using BMC diesels.

In international terms, it was felt that most of Britain's vehicle makers were too small to be able to attract overseas dealers or customer awareness and, indeed, many did not make left-hand-drive vehicles – Atkinson's first came in late 1949, for example. One way round this problem of acceptability was to fit the widely respected Perkins diesels to many of them and to make use of that company's worldwide spares and servicing organisation. Seddon was an advocate, as were newcomers

Owing to its adherence to Perkins diesels and competitive pricing, Seddon remained popular at home and abroad but was rarely encountered in Britain with normal control.

Proctor and Rutland (also called Manton and MTN in some countries). Leyland and AEC were large enough to command international attention and to be able to produce long runs of similar vehicles built from their own components. An example was the 1947 Comet 'world truck', named in honour of Leyland's work on the Comet tank. This had American-influenced styling in an attempt to compete with American vehicles, and it helped to push exports to 42 per cent of Leyland's 6,291-chassis output in 1949.

AEC showing its export credentials in 1953. In some markets its vehicles were known as ACLO.

Of the whole industry's grand total of lorry output for 6-ton loads and over, 2,418 of the 6,663 produced in 1930 were exported. In 1955 the figure was 9,853 exported out of 24,273, and in 1960 it was 27,101 out of 64,893.

Considering that total output of each of the smaller firms was rarely above one or two thousand per year, one can see why the efforts of the biggest firms were so important. They, and indeed their smaller rivals, explored every possible market niche, one of the largest being burgeoning quarry and construction businesses.

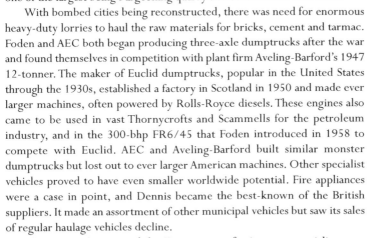

Kew Dodge sold its vehicles through three different dealer networks. Here is the Kew Fargo in Danish publicity, and there was also Kew De Soto.

With bombed cities being reconstructed, there was need for enormous heavy-duty lorries to haul the raw materials for bricks, cement and tarmac. Foden and AEC both began producing three-axle dumptrucks after the war and found themselves in competition with plant firm Aveling-Barford's 1947 12-tonner. The maker of Euclid dumptrucks, popular in the United States through the 1930s, established a factory in Scotland in 1950 and made ever larger machines, often powered by Rolls-Royce diesels. These engines also came to be used in vast Thornycrofts and Scammells for the petroleum industry, and in the 300-bhp FR6/45 that Foden introduced in 1958 to compete with Euclid. AEC and Aveling-Barford built similar monster dumptrucks but lost out to ever larger American machines. Other specialist vehicles proved to have even smaller worldwide potential. Fire appliances were a case in point, and Dennis became the best-known of the British suppliers. It made an assortment of other municipal vehicles but saw its sales of regular haulage vehicles decline.

The Rootes Group used the Karrier name for its more specialist types and tried heavier vehicles following its acquisition of Tilling-Stevens and its new subsidiary, Vulcan, in 1949. The most successful result was that Tilling-Stevens built Rootes's opposed two-stroke TS3 diesel used by Commer for over fifteen years.

Two-stroke diesels had mainstream endorsement from General Motors in the Second World War, and its Detroit diesels were widely used in post-war American transport. In Britain, Foden developed its own two-stroke but still found that most customers wanted Gardners.

Sentinel came up with an impressive underfloor diesel-engined range but managed to sell only 1,200 of them by 1956, when Rolls-Royce converted the factory to build its diesel engines. Ten years later came its Eagle range of automotive diesels, which carried on using the model name even after takeover by Perkins.

Another diesel to threaten Gardner's dominance amongst the smaller producers of custom-built haulage chassis was the American firm Cummins. It established a factory in Scotland to supply Euclid, which had become a General Motors company in 1953. Seddon offered Cummins diesels in its late-1950s heavyweights and these engines found many other customers for export vehicles and for the increasing requirements of higher speeds encouraged by the 1960s motorway network. Payloads and vehicle size were growing too after the government's Motor Vehicles (Construction and Use) regulations came into force in 1955. These allowed 8-foot-wide and 30-foot-long lorries to gross 14 instead of 12 tons on two axles, 20 instead of 19 tons on three axles and 24 instead of 22 tons on four axles.

Meanwhile, what of the hard-pressed British haulier? Things had changed dramatically in 1948 when the new Labour government nationalised the railways and long-distance road haulage, bringing them under centralised control. The Road Haulage Executive henceforth traded as British Road Services (BRS), with a new red livery for the 8,208 vehicles and 1,717 trailers that had been acquired with the 248 haulage businesses compensated by the end of 1948. Holders of C licences and strictly local operations were broadly excluded from this scheme, which led to massive growth in these areas.

In the face of mass-produced competition, Dennis found it increasingly difficult to remain in the mid-weight market from the mid-1950s, though it prospered with refuse collectors and fire appliances.

Aveling-Barford's answer to Foden, AEC and Euclid was the 27–35-ton SN of 1958, which came to have a choice of Rolls-Royce or Detroit diesels up to 476 bhp, and constant-mesh six-speed or automatic gearboxes.

BRS established depots all over the country and in 1950 employed a staff of 75,540. Its vehicle fleet reached a peak of 41,265 in 1952 but its days were numbered when the Conservatives returned to power in October 1951. They reasoned that nationalised transport was unwieldy and that the previous haulage companies had been more adaptive to market trends. Rail integration had not worked and British Railways racked up colossal losses for the next ten years.

BRS was permitted to carry on in slimmed-down form alongside the returning private hauliers and made a number of interesting innovations to become profitable. Several of the nationalised railway companies had bus interests, and one of them indirectly controlled the Bristol Tramways & Carriage Company, which had built lorries in the 1910s and 1920s but was best known for buses. From 1952 to 1958 it made 517 Leyland-engined rigid eights for BRS, and between 1955 and 1964 it built 651 examples of 24-ton artics powered by Leyland or Gardner engines. With the end of lorry production, buses continued and Leyland took a 25 per cent stake in the firm.

An interesting feature of many of the Bristols was the use of fibreglass in the cab construction, which in 1955 was said to save a

The forward-control Commer had a petrol engine canted to the side for a level cab floor but soon gained the revolutionary TS3 diesel.

The 1953 Thornycroft Sturdy Star 5/6-tonner was one of the first to feature the Motor Panels steel cab.

quarter of a ton in unladen weight. This new wonder material made styling changes relatively easy and inexpensive for small production runs, and many other lorries began to feature 'plastic' cabs. These were usually built on traditional ash frames, as used with metal-panelled cabs. For export, all-metal cabs were becoming essential for safety reasons (Sweden in particular adopted strict safety testing of cabs), and to discourage termites in the tropics. One might have thought that cabs that tilted for maintenance would also have been a high priority since they had been re-adopted in the United States, where White embraced the old idea in 1949, and Diamond T and International soon afterwards. The bodybuilder Neville, of Mansfield,

A 1956 Austin artic with Willenhall cab compared with its stylish 1959 replacement (opposite page, top), both powered by 5.1-litre BMC diesels.

Nottinghamshire, adopted the idea at the same time as White and converted some wartime normal-control Bedfords to forward control with this feature. They also converted Guy and other lorries to tilt, but customer uptake was slow and the concept did not achieve factory availability until 1962, initially with Foden.

The smaller makers could not afford the tooling to produce steel-framed cabs, and into the breach in 1952 stepped Motor Panels of Coventry with a standard cab that was adopted by several firms, including Thornycroft and Guy, with subtle styling differences on the front pressings. The Willenhall Radiator & Motor Pressings Company made other standardised cabs, used by BMC and Guy, but there was still room for individual flair for the lorries used in Britain, as ERF was to prove in the mid-1950s with its futuristic Kleer Vue cab featuring wrap-around windscreens. In 1958 Guy fitted much of its range with an equally avant-garde plastic cab with pronounced windscreen peak, and Atkinson adopted the wrap-around screen, though still with a traditional exposed radiator.

Also in 1958 Leyland, Albion and Dodge pooled resources to pay for the press tooling for Motor Panels' appropriately initialled 'LAD' metal cab. 135,000 were built over the next fifteen years.

The small specialist makers were joined by many other post-war hopefuls such as AWD, Douglas, Rotinoff and, at the end of Sentinel's lorry-making existence, the TVW, but few lasted for long. It was becoming very difficult for small firms now that the mass-producers were beginning to encroach on

Albion had belonged to Leyland for five years when this beer tanker was built in 1956, but it was still largely a Scottish product.

A rival to the giant Thornycroft, Scammell and Atkinson heavy haulage tractors of the 1950s was the Rolls-Royce six- or eight-cylinder powered Rotinoff, built near Heathrow Airport.

their territory with heavier vehicles. Bedford, which sold its half-millionth vehicle in 1947, had started the trend with heavier vehicles including a 5-tonner and an artic unit with Scammell automatic coupling and trailer. Then in 1950 came the S model, the so-called 'Big Bedford', a 7-tonner with forward control and synchromesh gearbox, the latter an unheard-of feature for a 'heavy'. From 1952 this could have a Leyland diesel, and Perkins diesels were soon available in smaller models.

Many vehicles of the 1950s had Eaton two-speed axles, an effective way of doubling the ratios available from a conventional gearbox.

Morris-Commercial had also gone up-market with a 1948 5-tonner powered by the firm's own four- and six-cylinder diesels based on Saurer patents covering the highly efficient Dual Turbulence combustion system. They sold over thirty thousand, with widespread exports.

The 'Big Bedford' 7-tonner had a Chevrolet look about it and featured such novelties as synchromesh and hydraulic brakes (initially hydro-mechanical in 1950).

Another important newcomer was Ford's Thames Trader of 1957, which had a stylish forward-control steel cab and Ford's own petrol or diesel engines, with four-speed synchromesh gearboxes. They became the popular basis of low-frame and off-road conversions by County and AWD. For regular haulage, they challenged Bedford's dominance in the tipper and other fields.

As these and other big firms made heavier vehicles, they forced Guy, Thornycroft and others out of the mid-weight field into the smaller volumes of specialist and heavy lorries. Thornycroft had made everything from the 100-ton Mighty Antar to the 3-ton Nippy but was struggling by the time that AEC came to its rescue in the early 1960s.

Above: Thornycroft sold over 750 Mighty Antars in the 1950s and early 1960s. They were originally developed for the Iraq Petroleum Company and soon became widely used for military tank transport.

Above: A French-language brochure illustration for the Thames Trader, new in 1957, with Ford's own petrol or diesel engines and synchromesh. 122,000 of this cab style were built up to the last in 1965.

Below: This 1959 Scammell Super Constructor had all-wheel drive and a 237-bhp Rolls-Royce diesel. It could tow in excess of 100 tons.

F86 with semi-trailer dumper body for building site and off-road work.

F86 6x2 with rigid platform hauling building stone.

LOADS OF POWER IN EUROPE

T HE BRITISH commercial-vehicle industry entered the 1960s bigger than all its rivals in France, Germany and Italy combined. Twenty years later it was only a third of their size. Many factors contributed to this sorry state of affairs, several of which could be squarely laid at the door of politicians. Their intervention saw the successful Leyland Group bogged down in a disastrous 1968 merger with the totally different type of mass-production business built up by BMC. In this hotchpotch was the Jaguar, Daimler and Guy group, Jaguar having moved into the commercial-vehicle field in 1960. Guy had launched its successful Motor Panels steel-cabbed Big J (for Jaguar) range in 1964 and sold well over five thousand of them. However, in the new British Leyland set-up they competed with several other brands and were axed in the late 1970s.

Another volume producer to have failed as a result of the gradual loss of distant export markets and some unsuccessful cars was the Rootes Group, which Chrysler began to buy into in 1964, achieving complete control by 1973. Again there was internal competition, this time between Commer and Dodge, and from 1976 the Commando range, new two years earlier, and other models became solely Dodges, apart from a few municipal Karriers. In 1978 loss-making Chrysler pulled out and Citroën-Peugeot took over. They produced Dodges until 1981, when Renault bought the commercial-vehicle interests; they sold Renault-badged Commandos and assembled some true Renaults until closure in 1993.

Meanwhile government meddling had seen both Rootes and BMC persuaded to build new factories in areas of high unemployment in Scotland. The former built cars and light vans at Linwood, Renfrewshire, while from 1961 BMC 'heavies' were built in Bathgate, West Lothian, and became Leylands in 1970. In marked contrast to the high-quality Albions from nearby Scotstoun, they were bedevilled with assembly problems and industrial unrest, and in 1975 the entire British Leyland operation had to be bailed out with government aid. Two years earlier, Leyland had launched its premium Marathon range, but this used a version of the tilt cab first seen in the 1964

Opposite:
Volvo was second to Foden in introducing tilt cabs in Europe in 1963, and the F86 led the conquest of the British market. This six-wheeler of 1972 dates from the year in which the five-thousandth Volvo entered British service with Smith's Crisps in September.

The FG series of BMCs, launched in 1959, had a so-called 'Threepenny Bit' cab, resembling the twelve-sided 3d coin of the time. An advantage for local delivery work was that the doors opened within the overall vehicle width.

Ergomatic range and was not modern enough to stem the tide of European imports.

The arrival of all these Mercedes-Benz, Fiat, Scania, Volvo, DAF and other vehicles was indirectly caused by politicians, but primarily by bad management and working practices. The political element was the result of European harmonisation, initially the 1964 Construction and Use Regulations, which increased maximum weight from 24 to 32 tons (with rigid eights allowed 28 tons with impracticably long wheelbases) and raised the legal speed to 40 mph (with no limit on the expanding motorway network). Unfortunately, the lorry industry was not given advance warning of the changes and lacked adequately powerful trucks to meet the new requirements.

The traditional hand-built British heavyweight from Foden, Atkinson and ERF typically had a rather basic cab interior with 150-bhp Gardner diesel and sliding-mesh 'crash' gearbox. The continentals brought greater power, often from turbocharged engines. They had comfortable cabs, with sleeping arrangements carefully considered (not tagged on as an afterthought), and many featured synchromesh to make driving easier.

British heavyweights began to adopt American-designed (but mostly British-built) drive trains consisting of Lipe clutches, Spicer propeller shafts,

The LAD cab laid bare to reveal a 1961 Leyland Super Comet with 400S Power-Plus diesel. The Albion and Dodge versions had subtle styling differences.

Left: The Leyland Group Ergomatic tilt cab was new in 1964 and is shown here on a 205-bhp AEC Mammoth Major 8 with six-speed gearbox and power steering.

Eaton and Fuller gearboxes (the latter with three ranges), and Rockwell axles (made in the Maudslay factory). Cummins made engines of adequate power output in Britain and these were adopted, leaving Gardner, with its beautifully engineered and expensive traditional sixes, out in the cold. Indeed, to provide higher power, Gardner made a straight eight but it was too long to fit under most cabs.

Perkins, which had tried turbocharging from 1962, introduced a V8 that went into Leyland Redline (as the Scottish variety was known to distinguish it from the upmarket Bluelines) and Dodge, notable in the latter's K-series heavyweights from 1965. In 1964 Perkins was making 1,200 engines per day,

Above right: The BMC tilt cab in action in 1964 artwork. In practice, the steering column had to be unbolted for tilting, and the side-flow radiator led to overheating.

Left: Leyland's top-of-the-range Marathon of 1973 envisaged operation in Britain at 38 tons but this did not happen until 1983. Here a double-trailer outfit, illegal in Britain, poses at the AEC factory in 1978 (when Rolls-Royce and Cummins largely replaced the AEC-designed engines in most earlier types).

Above: Cover of a 1965 catalogue issued by the bodybuilder Garner showing the contemporary Commer forward-control cab. Garner had offered complete lorries, originally of United States origin, from the First World War until 1942.

Below: A Foden with 1960 York registration and its maker's S20 coachbuilt cab conveys a Glasgow tram for preservation. Gardner or Foden's own two-stroke diesels were available at the time.

Above: Atkinson still featured its traditional aluminium radiator surround in 1967, complete with wooden-framed cab. Note its 'big A' and 'Knight of the Road' trademark, along with the Cummins badge.

but by then the company belonged to Massey-Ferguson and so was also heavily involved with farm tractors around the world.

In 1960 a 262-bhp Cummins had shown the practicability of maximum-weight operation at 70 mph in a Norde articulated outfit. This and a few other Nordes with American Hendrickson rubber suspension were built by a haulier but did not enter regular production. However, engines of similar output soon became widespread and were available to traditional assemblers from both Cummins and Rolls-Royce, with its Eagle range, launched in 1966 from the former Sentinel factory. Apart from Norde, the only other significant newcomers in the period were the late 1970s Dennison, made from British components in Ireland, and the Perkins-powered and Scottish-built Argyle from the late 1970s – neither of which achieved more than passing success. The Rowe Hillmaster fizzled out in Cornwall in 1962 after nine years of minimal sales and was the last of the regional makers.

Unipower and Shelvoke & Drewry had both been making specialist vehicles since before the Second World War but attempts at more mainstream products were made from the mid-1970s and failed.

Meanwhile, what of the more familiar British lorry makers? Seddon had bravely entered the semi-mass-production market in 1964 with the Perkins-6.354-powered 13/4 for 13 tons gross on four wheels (across the industry the twins at the rear always counted as singles when describing four-, six- or eight-wheelers). The 13/4 had a steel Supa-cab made by Motor Panels, which came to be used on heavier types powered by Perkins V8 and other engines. Seddon also made some traditional Gardner-, Cummins- and Leyland-powered models with cabs of plastics, but these had all gone by the time that it acquired Atkinson in 1970.

Another liaison had come in 1973 when Seddon tried to europeanise some models by installing Deutz air-cooled diesels. Little came of this project, though more successful was Seddon's assembly of Magirus-Deutz

The last of the completely Kew-designed Dodges was the five-speed K series of the mid-1960s, powered by a Cummins (later Perkins) engine, and which had a tilt cab exclusive to the model. Most would be replaced in the Chrysler range in 1975 by a Spanish Barreiros, renamed Dodge.

the amazing new **TK**

BEDFORD TK
FORWARD CONTROL

● 14 different chassis for payloads from 3 tons to 12 tons.
● Cab-ahead-of-engine design.
● Flat floor, walk-through, three-man cab.
● Grandstand vision, plus rear quarter windows.
● Extra low step-in height.

BETTER BUY BEDFORD...

all-wheel-driven on/off-road lorries up to 1970. Atkinson, too, had a German dalliance, using some steel cabs from the former Krupp lorry range in 1968. AEC had looked to Europe as well and at the time it joined Leyland in 1962 it also acquired French lorry maker Willème, which additionally assembled some BMC models. It was not a success and nor were the links with Vanaja in Finland and Barreiros in Spain, nor Leyland's links with Verheul in Holland, Brossel in Belgium and other international collaborations. By coincidence it was DAF, which had employed Leyland technology in the 1950s, that eventually came to the aid of the British company after General Motors had failed to buy it in 1986. GM had then shut down its own Bedford operation (allegedly in disgust at the political shenanigans), an incredible outcome when one considers that in 1960 Bedford had built 100,000 commercials in a single year for the first time, of which two-thirds had been exported, and had introduced its market-leading TK model.

Perhaps the most familiar lorry of this era was the Bedford TK from 1960. It was joined by larger KM versions in 1966 and the tilt-cab TM in 1972. Amazingly, the TK itself did not tilt until 1980, when it was redesigned as the TL.

In a desperate attempt to catch up with Continental thinking, Atkinson adopted the Krupp steel tilt cab in 1968 but stuck with home-grown Rolls-Royce 220-bhp diesels.

Leyland-DAF existed from 1987 and was bought in 1996 by the American group Paccar, whose brands included Kenworth, Peterbilt and, since 1980, Foden. Seddon and Atkinson came up with the rationalised 200 and 400 series tilt-cab ranges in the mid-1970s and were making some three thousand vehicles per year under the American ownership of International Harvester, which had bought Seddon-Atkinson in 1974. International had British farm-tractor assembly facilities and had used those at Doncaster to make American-specification medium trucks between 1965 and 1969. The American involvement, as with Chrysler at the Rootes Group, spelled disaster when there was a worldwide financial slowdown, and International Harvester, having also partly bought Pegaso in Spain in 1981 (another company based on Leyland technology), pulled out of Europe. International Harvester had also owned a stake in DAF and had sold Seddon-Atkinson to Pegaso in 1983. The Fiat-Ford-created Iveco group then bought Pegaso, including Seddon-Atkinson, in 1990.

However, all was not gloom and doom in Britain in the 1960s and 1970s. Ford had introduced its immensely successful tilt-cab D Series to replace the Thames Traders in 1965. This, in turn, gave way to the international Cargoes of 1981, after 540,000 D Series had been sold. In 1975 Ford had come up with a rival to Bedford's 1974-announced TM topweight range. This was the Transcontinental, which put Ford, like Bedford, in virtually every transport category, to the chagrin of the traditional suppliers. Cummins engines of up to 355 bhp were available by 1978, and assembly, using a Renault-Berliet cab, initially took place in Amsterdam before transfer to Foden's massively

Seddon-Atkinson's European truck was the 400, launched at the 1974 Amsterdam Show. It helped to take its share of the British market over 28 tons to above 20 per cent during 1975.

49

Foden's massive factory modernisation and expansion were ill-timed and led to the company's temporary downfall in 1979. The brand lasted to 2006, latterly at Paccar's Leyland factory. The S10 cabs shown were new in 1978.

expanded modern facilities at Sandbach, Cheshire. These produced military vehicles and a new European range that was expensive to develop and poorly received, and a key cause of receivership in 1979 and the subsequent Paccar rescue. Foden's output slumped from 1,340 in 1980 to 630 in 1983.

Foden's neighbour, ERF, was progressing better. Its rationalised A range of 1970 and B range four years later helped it build almost two thousand vehicles a year by 1980, and double that by the end of the decade. It retained its independence until purchase by MAN of Germany in 2000.

The Trans-continental, introduced in 1975, was Ford's answer to the continental invasion. A mixture of international components with British Cummins engine, it was assembled in Holland, and later at the Foden factory. Production of a thousand per year had dwindled to none by 1984.

MAN was one of several importers to tackle the rigid-eight market, formerly the preserve of British manufacturers. This is a 1976 30.232 DHK.

Dennis made a final attempt to stay in the heavy market with its Maxims, new in 1964. Many of these used a 185-bhp V8, which was one of Cummins's few unsuccessful introductions. Operators avoided it in much the same way that they mistrusted Leyland's much-vaunted Fixed Head 500 series of 1968.

The Maxim range was not a commercial success and ended Dennis's days in the mainstream. This Cummins diesel 6x4 carries a concrete mixer powered by a donkey engine.

A 1972 Routeman
Scammell powered
by a Rolls-Royce
Eagle engine.

This was built with cylinder heads cast in-unit with their blocks to obviate gasket problems, but it led to other overheating difficulties. Although many gave no trouble, they earned Leyland a poor reputation that was not overcome until it joined DAF. (Nowadays, Leyland builds trucks for DAF and others in the Paccar group.)

Within the Leyland Group, Scammell continued with its specialist vehicles and took over some of Thornycroft's designs. Its regular highway models, especially its rigid eights, remained important, particularly after the Routeman received a new low-weight plastics cab in 1962, styled by Michelotti, who also created the angular Triumph Herald car. The Scammell cab was nicknamed the 'Cheese Grater' on account of the pronounced strengthening ribs moulded into its front and sides, and it came to be used on several different Scammells. Meanwhile the bonneted Highwayman, with roots going back to the 1920s, lasted until soon after the arrival of the two- and three-axle Crusader in 1968. This had the universal Motor Panels cab and was conceived for long-distance haulage around the world. Rolls-Royce

This spectacular
outfit was in use
by JCB in 1966.
The ERF 66CU220
had a 220-bhp
Cummins diesel,
and gross weight
was 32 tons.

Eagles, Detroit two-strokes or V8s by Cummins or AEC were specified, but the majority went to the slimmed-down and part-privatised BRS in Eagle 220-bhp 4x2 form. To the annoyance of Leyland, it proved to be a serious rival to its Marathon and had to be built in the Guy factory to keep pace with demand.

In 1980 Leyland pinned all its hopes on the entirely new T45 Roadtrain with cab styled by Ogle, and followed it in 1984 with a smaller version called Roadrunner. Ogle had also had a hand in the Seddon-Atkinson 200 and 400 cabs. Although the Leylands were a match for the best of the world's trucks, they came too late to restore Leyland's fortunes as an independent business. The problem lay not in the vehicle but in that importers had made significant inroads into fleets up and down the British Isles.

Commercial-vehicle imports grew from 193 in 1950 to 2,919 in 1960, 10,317 in 1970 and 73,730 in 1980, although many of these were light vans rather than heavy lorries. By the late 1980s around 40 per cent of commercial-vehicle sales in Britain were of overseas origin.

In 1981 British new vehicle registrations, rather than production, in round figures consisted of:

Leyland, 7,000
DAF, 1,600
ERF, 1,600
Foden, 500
Ford, 10,500 (plus 180 from
    Holland)
Bedford, 7,400
Iveco, 1,700 (of which 600 were
    Magirus-Deutz)

Dodge, 4,900 (including 370
    Renaults)
MAN, 750
Mercedes-Benz, 2,500
Scania, 900
Seddon-Atkinson, 2,000
Volvo (Sweden), 2,000
Volvo (British-assembled), 634

In 1970 the 1,722 imported vehicles over 5 tons unladen weight consisted mostly of Volvos, and British firms accounted for 36,281 (including 15,081 from the Leyland Group) in this weight category. Something had gone badly wrong for British manufacturers during the decade and matters did not improve.

The creeping tide of heavy-vehicle imports included Mercedes-Benz, Scania and Volvo, tried by BRS. Up to 1975 its Midland Region fleet was entirely British but in that year a quarter of its intake was foreign.

By far the most important of these was Volvo, whose Swedish makers had investigated exports to Britain in the early 1960s and decided that the competition was too intense. Then a disaffected Scottish haulier named Jim McKelvie was so fed up with the inadequate spares and servicing facilities for his fleet and the nonchalant attitude of manufacturers that he

Scania's new 110
awaiting delivery
in Britain in 1968.
These had 11-litre
212-bhp six-
cylinder diesels
that could be
turbocharged
to 281 bhp.
Five-speed
synchromesh
gearboxes could
have epicyclic
splitters giving
ten ratios.

approached Volvo. He explained that with a good vehicle and faultless backup he could create a success. 185 examples of the F85 were imported in 1967 and the figure had grown to two thousand in 1972, by when five thousand were in use. By 1975 Volvo was market leader above 29 tons, and in 1984 there were 34,000 Volvo commercials on British roads. As Volvo and Scania had between them made a grand total of only 17,850 lorries in 1960 and 29,030 in 1970, this was no mean achievement. Scania chose the direct export route to achieve its more modest early success, but Volvo through McKelvie set up production facilities at Irvine in Ayrshire, where special models such as rigid eights could be tailored. Operators were initially suspicious of the potential longevity of the F86 small-capacity diesel, displacing only 6.7 litres yet developing over 200 bhp, thanks to turbocharging (an art pioneered by Volvo in 1954). Cummins relied on 14 litres for its classic 240-bhp power plant, and Gardner on similar capacity for its largely impractical 240-bhp straight eight – its 6LXB 10.5-litre engine developed only 188 bhp.

In the event, operators' fears proved groundless and, in any case, they were reassured by the existence of 536 service points across Europe and a round-the-clock dedicated rescue line promising to plot position and get help underway within ten minutes. With growing international haulage, operators needed vehicles with trans-European backup, something that the smaller British makers could not hope to achieve.

Having stormed Britain (and, indeed, the rest of Europe), Volvo next set its sights on North America and, in 1981, achieved the apparently impossible task of acquiring White Autocar, followed by GMC's heavy-vehicle division five years later.

Volvo's European rivals achieved similar success in Britain, but factors common to all were their perceived reliability, with resultant lack of downtime, and the fact that they were pleasant to drive for hours on end.

Volvo's larger LB76 model and the F88 that replaced it in 1968 had twin-range five-speed synchromesh gearboxes. Early in the F88's life, the inconvenient second lever for the splitter (also found on Fodens and others) was replaced by a button controlling the epicyclic split by air actuation. In 1970 the 330-bhp F89 arrived with a similar cab to the F88, both of which were much larger than on the F86 and in 40-cm-deeper sleeper form incorporated a wardrobe, extensive insulation, carpeting, a radio and comprehensive heating and ventilation controls. Naturally, the cab tilted but an extra requirement was that the radiator was also hinged. All controls were finger-light or servo-assisted.

Many British lorries were viewed by drivers as 'bosses' motors', intended to make a profit with scant regard to the comfort and well-being of the occupant of the cab. This marked the beginning of an era in which drivers helped to choose their vehicles and therefore felt more involved and committed to the future success of road haulage.

The era of truly international transport opened with Volvo's Globetrotter cab of 1979, shown here on an F12, a 330–385-bhp powered chassis first seen in 1977 and available with intercooled turbocharging within two years.

INDEX

Page numbers in italics refer to illustrations

ACV 32
ADC 16, *17*
AEC (ALCO) 11, 12, 15, 16, *16*, 17, *17*, 22, 23, 24, 26, 28, *28*, 31, 32, 33, 34, *34*, 35, 37, 40, *45*, 48, 53
Albion 11, *12*, 17, *27*, 28, 31, 33, 39
Argyle *8*, 47
Armstrong-Saurer 22, *23*
Atkinson 23, 31, 34, 39, 44, *46*, 47, 48, *48*, 49, 54
Austin 8, 14, 29, 31, 33, *38*, 39
Autocar 55
Aveling 23, 35, *37*
AWD 39, 40
Barreiros 47, 48
Bean 15
Beardmore 13, 17, 25
Bedford *25*, 26, 29, 31, *32*, 39, 40, *40*, 48, *48*, 49, 53
Benz 4, 23
Berliet 49
Blackstone 23
BMC 33, 39, 43, *44*, 45, 48
Bristol 37
Brossel 48
BRS 19, 32, 36, 37, 53
Burrell 7
Caledon 17, 23
Carrimore 12
Chenard-Walcker 13
Chevrolet 26, 31
Chrysler *35*, 43, 47, 49
Citroen 43
Clayton 7
Commer 7, *9*, 11, 16, 17, 25, 26, *26*, 28, 35, *37*, 43, *46*
County 40
Coventry Climax 25
Crossley 29, 32
Cummins 36, 45, 46, 47, 49, 50, 53, 54

DAF 44, 48, 49, 52, 53
Daimler 4, 5, 6, 11, 16, 31, 43
David Brown 24
Dennis *5*, 6, 7, 11, 28, 35, *36*, 51, *51*
Dennison 47
Detroit 35, 37, 53
Deutz 47, 53
Diamond T 38
Diesel, Dr Rudolf 22
Dodge 12, 24, 26, 27, *35*, 39, 43, 45, *47*, 53
Dorman 23
Douglas 39
Easyloader 14
Eaton 40, 44
ERF 24, 29, *29*, 39, 44, 50, *52*, 53
Euclid 35, 36, 37
Fiat 44, 49
Foden 7, *18*, 22, 23, 35, 37, 39, 43, 44, *46*, 49, 50, *50*, 53, 55
Ford 12, *12*, 17, 31, *32*, 40, *41*, 49, *50*, 53
Fowler 7, 23
Fuller 44
FWD 11, 12, 13
Gardner 22, 23, 24, 27, 28, 29, *30*, 35, 37, 44, 45, 46, 47, 54
Garford 12
Garner 24, *46*
Garrett 7, 17, 19, 23
General Motors (GMC) 12, 26, 27, 31, 35, 36, 48, 55
Gilford 12, 24, *25*
Guy *cover*, 8, 16, 28, 29, 31, 39, 40, 43, 53
GV *19*
Halley *12*, 15, 17
Hallford 4, 11, 22
Hendrickson 47
Hillman 16
HSG 24
Humber 16
International 38, 49
Iveco 49, 53
Jaguar 2, 43
Jeffery 11
Jensen, JNSN 29

Karrier 8, 11, *14*, *16*, 28, 35, 43
Kenworth 49
Kerr-Stuart 23
Kirkstall 24
Krupp 48
Lancashire Steam 7
Latil 13,
Lauth-Juergens 16,
Leyland *6*, 7, 11, 12, 15, 17, *19*, *20*, 23, *24*, *27*, 28, 29, 33, 34, 37, 39, 40, 43, *44*, *45*, 45, 47, 48, 49, 50
Liberty *13*
Lifu 5
Lipe 44
Mack *12*
Magirus-Deutz 47, 53
MAN 50, *51*, 53
Mann 23
Manton (MTN) 34
Massey-Ferguson 47
Maudslay *1*, 8, 11, 31, 32, *33*, 45
McKelvie, J 53, 54
McLaren 23
Meadows 25
Mercedes-Benz 22, *22*, 44, 53
Michelotti 52
Milnes 6, 7
Moreland 14
Morris 14, *14*, 26, 31, 33, *33*, 40, 45
Motor Panels *38*, 39, 43, 47, 52
Napier *8*, 28
Nash 11
Neville 38, 39
Norde 47
Ogle 53
Opel 27, 31
Orwell 17
Paccar 49, 50, 52
Pagefield 22
Panhard 4
Peerless 12
Pegaso 49
Perkins 25, 34, 35, 40, 45, 47
Peterbilt 49
Petter 25

Proctor 34
Ransomes 17, 19
Renault 43, 49, 53
Reo 27, 29
Robey 7
Rockwell 45
Rolls-Royce 35, 37, 45, 47, 48, 52
Rootes 16, 26, 28, 31, 35, 43, 49
Rotinoff 39, *40*
Rowe 47
Rutland 34
Ryknield 8
S & D 14, *24*, 47
Salter Report 21
Saurer 4, 22, *23*, 26, 40
Scammell 12, 15, *15*, *28*, 28, 31, 33, 35, 40, *41*, *52*, 52
Scania 44, 53, 54, *54*
Seddon 29, 34, *34*, 36, 47, 49, *49*, 53
Sentinel 7, 17, *18*, 24, *24*, 35, 39, 47
Shefflex 25
Singer 15
Spicer 44
Star 16
Stevens 4, *5*
Stuart, HA 22
Sunbeam 8
Tangye 23
Thames 31, *32*, 40, 49
Thornycroft *3*, 4, 7, *7*, *10*, 11, 28, 31, 33, *38*, 39, 40, *41*, 52
Tilling-Stevens 4, 35
Trials 5, *6*, 7
Triumph 52
TVW 39
Unipower 47
Vanaja 48
Vauxhall 26
Verkeul 48
Volvo *42*, 43, 44, 53, 54, *55*
Vulcan 14, 35
White 38, 39, 55
Willème 48
Willenhall 39
Wolseley 8, 26, 31
Yorkshire Patent 23